finding

Zoya Hassan

BookLeaf Publishing

Presentation by *BookLeaf Publishing*

Web: www.bookleafpub.com

E-mail: info@bookleafpub.com

ISBN: 9789357212106

First edition 2023

DEDICATION

to everyone who is on a journey to love themselves-

the hardest part is falling, isn't it?

ACKNOWLEDGEMENT

First and foremost, I would like to thank Allah/God (SWT) for providing me with this opportunity. It was completely out of nowhere- it had randomly popped up on my stream on the day the admission was due, and I still remember running around my house before school telling my parents what the program was and how I really wanted to sign up. It was only because you willed me to find out about this that I did, and only because you willed me to sign up for this that I was able to, Alhumdulillah. Secondly, I would like to thank my parents for helping me sign up and actually following up to make sure I hadn't accidentally forgotten to keep writing (Ammi, Abbu and Bia- Jazakhallah!) And to Abbu, Adnan Chachoo and Atiya Phoppo- thank you all for going out and finding me a digital drawing pen. I'm really thankful that you guys made so much effort and went through different types to help find me one that suited my computer. I would also like to thank all my friends who always encourage me in my writing pieces, whether that be short stories I wrote for assignments or poems I write for myself. Honestly, I'm really glad that you guys put up with me. And finally, I would like to thank the person who made it possible for me to actually write these poems- you know who you are.

- silent but violent -

i stand here, silently
as my life cracks, violently
but i tell you i'm fine, though i'm lying

i stand here, silently
while you move on, violently
accepting my answer without prying

i stand here, silently
as the days go on, violently
and now, i've really stopped trying

yet i stand here, silently
as you break me, violently
leaving me, internally crying

and soon i'm standing here, silently
praying here, violently
for the day i overcome the challenge
dying.

- self-hate -

once again
i sorrow
for what it is to come
tomorrow

the same game
of lame shame
that we play, you and i

for once again
i will sit down when
the lights have all gone dark

and in the mirror,
you will smirk as i stare,
mocking our reflection.

i know this game
that we play
have memorized it by heart

because now you will crush
me in a rush
when you open your mouth

and say the words
that haunt me
day and night

and i will let it happen
without battin'
even so much as an eye

so this game will
go on as always
for this is not a phase

because the words you say
will once again weigh
heavily on my shoulders

i could try
i really could
to stop you
and i would

but i don't.

i let it happen.

for it is easier to do
with my mind askew
due to the constant chant of

"i
hate
you."

- self-doubt -

i
am
not
foolish enough

to think
she
likes
me

- reminders -

i
am
reminded of
how
i
was

- little girl -

last night i had a weird dream
in which i met
a little girl.

she had big eyes
and missing teeth,
and i remember she
stared up at me.

we were in my head
surrounded by the black
that now makes me "me"

she looked around,
then at the ground
and with a sigh, said

"what happened to us?
tell me this isn't real?"

i looked at her,
taking in the face
that looked so much
like mine

yet i turned away from my own
in regret of
how i'd grown

because
          what am i supposed to tell a little girl
                              who doesn't know she
eventually stopped trying?

so i twisted
and walked away
without saying a word

i did not want
to ruin her innocence
with the pointless struggles
of maturing

because yes,
it is true,

and there's
          no
            point
                in
                  lying.

- little girl pt.II -

dear little girl,
where have you gone?

have you run away
though you did nothing wrong?

did i scare you away
when i showed you my flaws?

or maybe i triggered
the last of your straws?

dear little girl,
was it something i said?

or maybe it was
everything in my head?

the hate, the sorrow,
the anger, the dread,

were you scared of all
the things i have bled?

dear little girl,

could you give me a chance?

do you think we can try
and save this mess of a dance?

would you run away
without so much of a glance?

or maybe could we try
for some self-romance?

dear little girl,
i am not all black.

yes i know,
there are things that i lack.

but with a little help,
we can get right on track.

so dear little girl,
please come back.

- self-doubt pt.II -

i miss you

but,

i am afraid.

- questions -

what if?
what if i showed you
my faults
and my struggles
my mistakes
and my failures?

would you look past them,
and see the real me?

or would you run away?

would you hold me close
and tell me
you loved me
even though
i myself do not?

despite all my flaws,
would you
stay
with
me?

- self-doubt pt.III -

i
am
not
brave

- trying -

heart pounding,
i forced myself
to face
myself
for the first time in a while.

breathing heavy,
i watched
as the monsters rose,
fangs beared
and claws drawn,
threatening to swallow me whole.

panicking,
i shut my eyes,
not wanting to watch
as they descended upon me,
and i realized that

facing myself
was much easier said
than done.

exhaling, i turned
around and walked out of the light

and into the dark.

i suppose
making peace with my demons
will
take
some
time

- again -

gritting my teeth,
i took in a breath.

it was time
to yet again
face myself.

breathing heavy,
i watched once again
as my monsters rose,
their fangs beared
and their claws drawn,
as they threatened to swallow me whole.

but i did not panic.
i did not turn away.

i planted my feet
and lifted my chin
and stared them straight in the eye.

i could feel
my heart pounding
and my body shaking.

but i would not run.
not again.

this time,
i will stare
and study
and learn.

because it is i
who brought these demons into existence.

and it is i
who has to live with them.

...so i might as well get comfortable.

- tried -

my palms are sweaty.
i am afraid.

and
it
is
beautiful.

- first step -

despite the mess
inside my heart,
it seems that i
have done my part
in taking a step
towards finding myself,
despite the mess
inside my heart.

- progress -

who knew learning to
love myself would be
so scary,
but so
so
so
worth it?

- you & i -

i guess
i always knew
what it was like
to look
in the mirror
and smile.

i suppose that
this whole time
i
was afraid
of whether or not
you
would smile back.

- reflection -

"i love you
 i love you
  i love you"

as i stared in the mirror,
and met my own gaze
i realized that,
indeed,
i loved her

- learned -

i always believed
love was a brilliant and enchanting thing
growing up i believed
that it was perfect.
filled with kind words and gentle touches
sweet gestures and late lunches
under a cloudless sky
with the sun shining bright above us.
i always believed
love was untouchable.

growing up i believed
that love was to be shared by lovers
and only lovers.

but i was wrong.

because over time i learned
that there is more to love
than romance.

it is soft and warm
among those you hold dear
it is exciting and amazing
with those you hold near

yet it is also pain
it is hate and hardship and struggle
and grief and anger and regret

because over time i learned
that the biggest battle
of love
is loving yourself
as you are

all your flaws
and your mistakes
your good parts
and bad parts
the things you pride
and the things you hide

self-love is ugly
it is tough and terrifying
and sometimes the hardest part is falling

but self-love is wonderful
because it is real

- mine -

b
r
o
k
e
n
as she is,

she
is
mine.

www.ingramcontent.com/pod-product-compliance
Lightning Source LLC
Chambersburg PA
CBHW062110140826
49812CB00058B/1214
9789357212106